The Picture Life of
JIMMY CARTER

BY BARBARA J. WALKER

FRANKLIN WATTS | NEW YORK | LONDON | 1977

THE PICTURE LIFE OF

Jimmy Carter

FOR MY FRIENDS LILIAN AND SAM REAVIN

Photographs courtesy of:
Charles M. Rafshoon: pp. 2-3, 6, 12, 14, 15 (left and right),
16-17, 22, 24, 25, 26-27, 29, 31, 33, 35, 36, 37, 38, 39,
44-45, 46, 47 (top left and right, bottom left);
World Wide Photos: pp. 8 (left and right), 9 (left and right),
10 (top and left), 11 (left and right), 18, 19, 21, 30, 41;
United Press International: pp. 10 (right), 32, 42, 47
(bottom right), 48.

Cover photograph: Charles M. Rafshoon

Library of Congress Cataloging in Publication Data

Walker, Barbara J.
    The picture life of Jimmy Carter.

    (Picture lives)
    SUMMARY: Text and photographs examine the
life and political career of the thirty-ninth President of
the United States.
    1. Carter, Jimmy, 1924-   — Juvenile literature.
2. Presidents — United States — Biography — Juvenile
literature. [1. Carter, Jimmy, 1924-   2. Presidents]
I. Title.
E873.W34   973.926'092'4 [B] [92]   77-368
ISBN 0-531-01284-0

6 5

The Picture Life of
JIMMY CARTER

"Hello. I'm Jimmy Carter. And I'm running for President."

Jimmy used to be sure of two things when he said that. Somebody would make a joke about his teeth. Someone else would say, "Jimmy who?"

There are still jokes about his big teeth. But now everybody knows Jimmy Carter, the peanut farmer from Plains, Georgia. He is President of the United States.

How did a man nobody knew get to be President? It was not easy.

Jimmy started running for President in 1974. That was two years before the election. He needed time to get to know the voters. They needed time to get to know him.

Florida

California

NEW LEADERSHIP & COMPETENCE

CARTER-MONDALE in '76

He visited barber shops, factories, supermarkets, and many more places. He traveled across the country. Jimmy didn't just want to win big in a few important cities and states. He was going to try to win everywhere.

Georgia

New York

Rosalynn
in Missouri

Miss Lillian
in New York

His family helped. Rosalynn, Jimmy's
wife, told the people that her husband
would make a good President. Jimmy's
mother, Miss Lillian, spoke to senior
citizens.

Chip in Delaware

Jeff in Michigan

His sons — Jack, Jeff, and Chip —
talked at picnics and country fairs. Amy,
Jimmy's eight-year-old daughter, wanted
to go everywhere with her father. But he
wouldn't let her miss school.

Jimmy told the voters, "I will speak up for you in Washington." He said he knew that most Americans wanted to work. But they could not find jobs. He said he knew what it meant to be poor. Jimmy promised to change things if he got to be President.

Jimmy Carter is a rich man. He grows and sells peanuts. He also sells peanuts grown by other farmers. His business makes over $800,000 a year. How is it that he could speak for the poor? Carter goes back to his childhood to tell why.

Jimmy working at
his peanut warehouse

Jimmy was born October 1, 1924. He was the first child of James Earl Carter, Sr., and his wife, Lillian. Jimmy was named after his father.

He has two sisters and one brother — Gloria, Ruth, and Billy. The Carter home was in Archery, three miles west of Plains.

Jimmy, age five, and his sister Gloria

Jimmy dressed for his part in a school play. He was ten years old.

James Earl Carter, Sr., was a hardworking farmer. Peanuts was one of his important crops. He also owned a store in Plains. And he sold many goods that came from the farm.

Jelly was made from the farm's fruit.
Wool from the farm's sheep was made into
blankets. Carter even made his own syrup.
He called it "Plains Maid."

Just how poor were the Carters?
Miss Lillian says they were not so bad off.
Water had to be pumped by hand. They
had no heat, except for fireplaces. They got
electric lights when Jimmy was sixteen.
But they always had enough to eat.

Ten-year-old Jimmy with his colt, Lady Lee.

Thirteen-year-old Jimmy with his dog, Bozo.

Jimmy worked hard on the farm. But he had his own business, too. He started it when he was five years old. Everyday he sold bags of boiled peanuts on the streets of Plains. He made about a dollar on weekdays. On Sundays he made about five dollars.

Jimmy saved his money until he was nine years old. Then he bought a few bales of cotton at a low price. A few years later, the price of cotton rose. Jimmy sold his bales for more money than he had paid for them.

Jimmy used his cotton money to buy five houses! He rented them. In all, he made $16.50 a month in rent.

Jimmy and some of his classmates. Jimmy is on the left holding the flag.

BUILDING FOR TODAY
AND TOMORROW

Jimmy was good at business. But he really wanted to do something else. He dreamed of being in the Navy like his uncle. Jimmy's uncle wrote to him from faraway places. He sent presents, too.

One day Jimmy wrote to the United States Naval Academy at Annapolis, Maryland. He asked how to go about getting in. Jimmy didn't tell them how old he was. And a good thing, too. He was still in elementary school!

The school sent Jimmy a booklet. He learned it by heart.

Jimmy's high school class.
Jimmy is the kneeling boy
at the end of the first row.

Jimmy at Annapolis

In 1943, Jimmy went to Annapolis. He graduated in 1946. Then his work began. He taught mathematics to Navy men. Part of Jimmy's work was going to school! The Navy wanted to build a new kind of submarine. One that could travel around the world without stopping for fuel. Scientists were needed to help plan the submarine. Jimmy became a nuclear engineer so he could help.

Except for short visits home, Jimmy did not go back to Plains for eleven years. One trip home was special. Jimmy went back to marry Rosalynn Smith, a local girl.

The Navy sent Jimmy and Rosalynn all over the country. Each of their four children was born in a different state.

Just married!

One thing happened in the Navy that Jimmy would never forget. His submarine was riding on the ocean surface one stormy night. Jimmy was standing watch on deck alone. Suddenly a giant wave swept him up with it into the air. He was almost carried into the ocean. He thought he would surely drown. But the wave crashed down onto the ship. Jimmy landed on top of a big gun. He was able to crawl back to his post.

Jimmy, facing the camera, on submarine number K-1

Jimmy left the Navy when his father died. He went back home to run things.

In 1954, the Supreme Court said that school segregation was against the law. The South was in an uproar over this. In Plains, the sheriff and the Baptist minister asked Jimmy to join the White Citizen's Council. This group believed whites and blacks should be kept apart. Jimmy was the only man in town who wouldn't join. People tried to get him to change his mind. They would not do business with him. Jimmy wouldn't give in. In time, people gave up the boycott.

The Plains Baptist Church

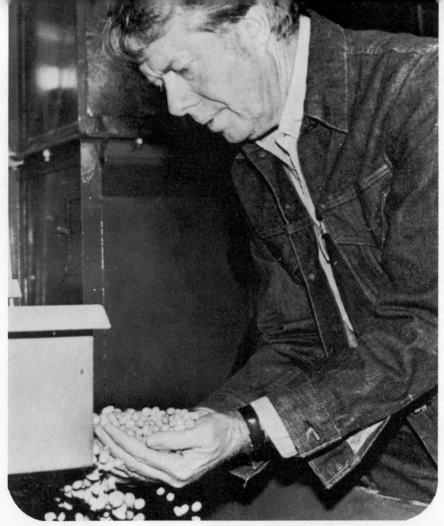

Checking a crop of shelled peanuts

This was not Jimmy Carter's only trouble at this time. He knew nothing about modern farming. Because of this his business was in bad shape. The first year he made less than $200.

Jimmy wanted to have a good business. So, he read books on farming. He talked to farmers. And he went back to school to learn more. His hard work paid off. The business grew. He made money.

Unloading a truck full of peanuts

Jimmy was not at first interested in politics. Then he was put on the school board. And he saw that being in office was a way to make changes for the good.

Politics began to take up more of Jimmy's time. His brother, Billy, came into the business to help.

Jimmy and his brother, Billy

Running for Governor

When Jimmy first ran for President, he
was known only by the people of Georgia.
Voters across the country were feeling
uneasy about him. They didn't know who
he was. What did he believe in? Would he
keep his promises? How could they find the
answers? Voters had to look at what he
had done in Georgia.

Jimmy was elected to the Georgia state senate in 1962. He served four years.

In the senate race Jimmy said he would read every bill before he voted on it. This meant reading eight hundred to a thousand bills! He had to learn to speed-read. But he kept his promise.

Jimmy likes to get out and meet the people. Sometimes he writes letters thanking people who voted for him.

Jimmy was elected Georgia's governor in 1970. He served four years.

Jimmy had promised not to govern behind closed doors. So he wrote a "sunshine" bill. It opened meetings to the people.

Jimmy as he became governor.
Amy was two years old at the time.

Jimmy in his office

Jimmy promised to save the state money. He did. Jimmy says he saved $53 million in one year! Some people say it was less than this.

Jimmy had said there were too many state agencies. He thought the state's business could be run just as well with less. So he cut the number from three hundred to twenty-two. Some workers lost their jobs. But not workers who were in the merit system. Those workers had passed a test to get their jobs. And Jimmy made sure they all kept them.

Governor Carter

He promised to help the handicapped. He gave them jobs. They took the place of police doing desk work. The police could go back to the streets where they were needed.

He began important changes in Georgia's prisons.

He fought for clean air and water.

The sign is right. Jimmy thinks many places in the wild should be left as they are.

Carter CARES ABOUT Conservation!

Did Carter keep all his promises by using kindness and love? One angry enemy said, "If you're not with him, he'll cut your throat!"

One thing is certain. There were no scandals while Carter was governor.

Jimmy at St. Simon's Island, Georgia.
He likes to go there to rest and think.

Jimmy Carter has promised the country many of the same things he promised the people of Georgia. The nation trusts he will be as good as his word.

The Plains railroad station.

The Carter family

1. James Earl Carter, Jr. (nicknamed Jimmy)
2. Rosalynn
3. Amy Lynn
4. Annette (Jeff's wife)
5. Jeffrey (nicknamed Jeff)
6. James Earl Carter, III (nicknamed Chip)
7. Caron (Chip's wife)
8. John William (nicknamed Jack)
9. Jason (Jack and Judy's son)
10. Judy (Jack's wife)

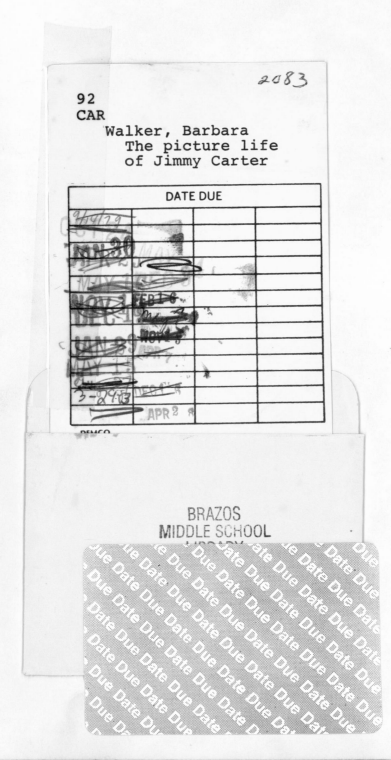

2083

92
CAR

Walker, Barbara
   The picture life
   of Jimmy Carter

DATE DUE			
9/14/79			
MAY 30			
MAY			
NOV	FEB 16		
DEC	May 3		
JAN 28	NOV 18		
MAY	MAY 7		
	DEC 1		
3-29-03	APR 2		

DEMCO